COGNITIVE BEHAVIORAL THERAPY

CBT for Beginners - 6 Proven Steps for Retraining Your Brain To Overcome Anxiety, Depression, Anger, PTSD, Panic Attacks, Worry, & More!

RAMIT GUPTA

Table of Contents

Introduction

Thank you and congratulations on your purchase of *Cognitive Behavioral Therapy – CBT for Beginners!* Since you purchased this book, you are likely going through a difficult period in your life and looking for a way to better cope on your own. Perhaps you went through some recent trauma, or you have been feeling anxious, or you have a phobia that is beginning to affect your quality of life. Regardless of why you picked up this book, you will find the support you need to begin restructuring your thinking and move forward in your journey toward a healthy mental state.

This book will guide you through the steps typically followed during cognitive behavioral therapy, which is a type of psychotherapy during which you work closely with a therapist to identify ways of thinking that are detrimental to your mental health. Typically, these are inaccurate or overall negative thoughts that are coloring your perception of the world and keeping you in a negative mindset. With cognitive behavioral therapy, you will go through the steps of identifying situations that are troubling you, becoming aware of how you feel about these troubling situations, and the core beliefs at the heart of your feelings. You will learn how to identify the harmful and inaccurate thinking associated with your core beliefs, and how to reshape your harmful and inaccurate thinking to better cope with troubling situations, hopefully clearing up any of the negative feelings that are weighing on you enough to feel like you need to seek help. In this book, you will also learn how to set goals that are important to your well-being and how to meet them. You will also get a brief overview of common obstacles you may face in your cognitive behavioral therapy journey, as well as some techniques to overcome them. Through following these steps, you will learn better coping skills that enable you to better handle traumatic or distressing events.

This sort of therapy is typically quite effective in the short-term reduction of stress and symptoms of mental health disorders, as well as long-term when the user makes a conscious effort to maintain and continue to utilize these skills in day-to-day life. By committing to the steps in this book, you will learn the basic skills taught as part of a typical cognitive behavioral therapy routine and how to apply them to any situation in your life that may be giving you trouble.

As you read this book and delve into your thoughts and feelings about some of the most traumatic times in your life, it is entirely normal to feel discomfort; you are literally parsing through your thoughts on a traumatic event or period of time to identify ways to change how you think about it. This process can be especially difficult, and many people find themselves discouraged or unwilling to work through the pain. However, just like with other major wounds, you must get through the pain to begin to heal. If at any point you feel as if you cannot cope or continue through the processes this book provides you, please seek third-party advice and do not be afraid to ask for help from friends and family. This book, while being a valuable source of information, provides general advice and cannot completely replace expert, customized advice you would receive through seeing a therapist. If you ever feel like you cannot handle your problem alone or are contemplating suicide, please locate your country's suicide hotline or your nearest emergency room for assistance.

STEP 1:

~

Identify the Problem

Life is full of ups and downs for everyone, and everyone goes through periods of stress in their lives. These periods are an integral part of being human. For many people, they take these periods in stride and get out of their funk relatively quickly without any lasting impact on their daily lives. Despite their stress, they are able to compartmentalize it while they continue to function, or they already have proper coping methods already that allow them to get by. For others, they find themselves unable to cope and fall into a state of depression or anxiety that they feel incapable of climbing out on their own. Maybe these people were never taught how to cope as children, or they encountered enough trauma that internalized the idea they would never be able to be prosperous and healthy, or they were merely born with a predisposition toward these negative thoughts, feelings, and states.

Regardless of the reason for it, some people may need an extra helping hand to get them back to a state of mental stability, and that is okay. Asking for help is not a sign of weakness, but it is an acknowledgment of being unable to do something and being brave enough to ask for assistance. This assistance could come in the form of learning how to cope healthily with stressors, such as in this book, or it could come in the form of therapy, changing lifestyle, and potentially with medication as well, as a last resort if the other methods do not work. This book will provide the methods used in cognitive behavioral therapy to teach you some of the ways to cope with your stress to try to correct depressive or anxious tendencies without the need for a therapist or medication. If this method does not work for you, you may need to pursue other methods as well.

The first step in the process toward healing your mental state is identifying the problem that is causing you distress. This chapter will teach you how to identify what stressor may be keeping you at a low point in your life, so you will be prepared to address the situation and achieve mental health.

It may be hard for you to pinpoint which stressors are just difficult periods of your life that you can get through on your own, and which are actual problems that will negatively impact your life to the point that you need help. When it feels like everything in life is wrong, it is often hard to find solid ground to begin, and every small misstep or stressor may seem to be much worse than it actually is, even when it is unrelated to the problem you wish to solve. These smaller stressors do not help your situation, but they are not the actual cause of your mental suffering. Some stressful problems may not seem easily fixable with these methods, such as a financial problem, but you can apply the skills learned in this book to almost any stressful situation in your life.

When considering issues you may be having in life, you need to first identify various stressors you are facing. Let's consider our new fictional friend, Jane. She is facing a vital work deadline that will enable her to get a promotion if she meets it and exceeds expectations. Her best friend has been busy and unable to talk as much as usual and has skipped their last few routine get-togethers. Money has been tight, so she really needs the raise she will get with the possible promotion. She has also been arguing with her fiancé about whether they will have children soon because he feels they don't have the money they would need to support a child despite Jane wanting one. All of this has culminated in Jane feeling overwhelmed and exhausted at all times. She avoids having conversations with her co-workers because she wants to meet her deadline, but when she tries to work, she is too busy thinking about her arguments with her fiancé to get anything done. Her best friend, whom she would usually speak to, is unreachable, so her usual method of reducing stress has failed. Jane finds herself trapped in a vicious cycle in which she desperately wants her fiancé to agree to have a child, but he won't agree until they have more money, and this stressor is causing her to be unable to focus at work. Even though she knows that doing well and getting the promotion will satisfy her fiancé's requirement that they make more money, she cannot bring herself to function because she is too preoccupied with the fact that there is an argument, to begin with. In this situation, the problem that needs to be addressed by Jane is the disagreement between her fiancé and herself over children and her perception of the situation. While it is distressing to not be able to speak to her friend, the fact that her friend is unavailable was not the root of her anguish or the primary cause of her spiral into disordered thinking. It may have added to some of her stress, but it was not directly responsible for the situation that she finds herself in. She does not think that she failed to meet her deadlines because her friend was not available, so that is not the root of her problem.

As an outsider to the situation without any emotional investment, it may be easy to merely tell Jane that if she worked hard and got the promotion, this entire argument would be a non-issue since the promotion would bring the money her fiancé wanted to have before considering children. If Jane were to sit down and think rationally about the situation, detaching her emotions from it, she would see the simple solution as well: Focus on work, get the promotion, and then revisit the conversation about having a child. However, her preoccupation with the fact that there is a conflict, to begin with, prevents her from thinking rationally and just fixing the problem while meeting her deadline. Instead, she wallows in self-pity at work in a self-defeating cycle that will inevitably cost her time, money, and potentially her relationship with her fiancé. She will miss her deadline at work, lose the possibility of getting a promotion, and her fiancé will remain firm on not having a child yet due to their financial situation remaining inadequate. This domino effect sends her spiraling further into her depression, yearning for a child that she could have potentially had and becoming fixated on why her fiancé would have said no, to begin with. Had she not been so caught up in her fiancé's answer of "Not right now, but let's re-evaluate in the future," she would have avoided this stress altogether. Soon, she begins to struggle to get out of bed, and starts avoiding going anywhere she might run into children, as seeing other women with children brings all of the negative feelings and insecurities about her fiancé she has back to the surface. Her work performance and attendance worsen, and she loses her job as a result. Unemployment makes the financial situation even worse, which causes her fiancé to double down on his convictions and table the talk of having children even longer, continuing the cycle.

In this case, Jane may be inclined to say that her fiancé is at fault. It is his fault she missed the deadline and ultimately lost her job, and it is his fault that she is spiraling into depression. Jane may get stuck in the mindset of thinking that if her fiancé had just agreed to have a child, none of this would have happened and life would be fine. This conclusion in her mind breeds resentment that negatively impacts her relationship even more. Any time she sees her fiancé, she feels resentful for their entire situation. If left unchecked, it could potentially destroy their engagement.

From a clinical standpoint, Jane is half right; the problem in this situation is that her fiancé believed that they did not have enough money for a baby and he was uncomfortable with the prospect of having a child without first bettering their financial situation. However, this does not mean that her fiancé was wrong in deciding to wait, or that the depression Jane faces is his fault. He did not cause her to miss her deadlines and did not cause her to lose her job. He holds no blame for these events occurring, but his actions certainly had enough of an effect on her to negatively impact her job. The problem here is subjective; it is whatever is causing the distress that is causing the symptoms, regardless of whether it is true or false, right or wrong, or rational or irrational. In this case, Jane's fiancé can be both completely without guilt from the situation while still being the root cause of it.

To identify the problem that needs fixing, you must first identify the causes of emotional distress, and the distress should meet specific criteria. Is the problem completely preoccupying you to the point you find yourself always thinking about it, regardless of what else you are or should be doing? Are you spending many of your waking hours dwelling on it to the point where you cannot accomplish what you need to? Is it interfering with your quality of life or your responsibilities? Do you have to change your lifestyle in order to accommodate the problem and avoid negative feelings? Do you find yourself taking up dangerous or destructive habits such as drinking, taking substances, or binge eating in order to cope with the situation? If you can answer yes to any of these, you may want to consider evaluating the situation to decide if you need new coping methods or if there may be another way of handling it that will be more productive and conducive to a healthier state of mind. If, at any time, you feel unable to stop the use of destructive methods to cope, such as drinking or taking illegal drugs, reach out to your doctor for resources that can help you. Your physician will be able to determine if you potentially need medical intervention or supervision to stop one of these coping mechanisms, as suddenly stopping drugs can cause your body to go through a dangerous period of withdrawal.

Revisiting Jane's predicament, you may recall that she was preoccupied as soon as her fiancé said he wanted to wait to have children, dwelling on what he decided for the both of them all day at work. After all, planning to have children is one of those decisions where both parties have to be completely on board, so when he said no, he made the decision for both of them. Dwelling on this interfered with her job as her deadline passed and her performance dropped, which ultimately interfered with her livelihood, and made their financial problem worse. She now finds herself with even less money for the child she desperately desires, and she still blames her fiancé for the entire situation, hurting her relationship. She has changed her lifestyle and the places she frequents to accommodate the problem in an attempt to avoid the negative feelings that will continue to fester until they are addressed, because every time she sees a child, all of her hurt and resentment rush back. All of these cumulate into one significant problem all rooted in the fact that her fiancé would prefer to wait to have children for a reason most people would consider logical and legitimate.

The problem you are facing and attempting to fix could be anything, so long as it negatively impacts your life and ability to function as a normal, productive member of society in a significant way. Maybe it is being extremely nervous around people, so you avoid any social interactions that are not entirely necessary and, consequently, your social life is virtually non-existent, and you cannot keep a job. Or perhaps you have a debilitating fear of birds, so you avoid leaving your home at all costs to avoid a panic attack when a sparrow flies over your head, or you hear a crow cawing. This fear negatively impacts your ability to work, socialize, and buy the things you need to live, as well as leaves you in a state of fear any time your curtains are open.

Regardless of whether the cause of distress is something that would be considered ridiculous or legitimate by the general public, it could be an actual problem worthy of addressing for you, and being a problem for you is the only legitimization it needs for therapeutic processes. Even patently false problems, such as the fear of looking into mirrors because you are afraid your reflection will kill you, are worthy of treatment and no less legitimate than the fear of cars after a severe car accident or a fear of the dark after being assaulted walking to your dorm at night.

The problems you face could also be events that have caused you trauma, such as growing up in an abusive home or your spouse cheating on you. These events and the ensuing trauma could shape your lifestyle negatively due to trying to avoid history from repeating itself. By trying desperately to avoid history repeating, you could find yourself stuck in a cycle of being unable to function. Maybe you never tell your significant other what you would prefer for dinner because a family member in the past constantly belittled you. By avoiding voicing your opinions and preferences, you feel like your needs and desires are not important, which plants the seeds for an ultimately false belief that you as a person are not valuable or worthy of consideration.

Another problem could be a bad habit, such as biting your nails or picking at your skin. These types of habits can cause real, physical harm and may also cause the person to feel embarrassed at the state of their skin. Even worse, it could be an eating disorder or a substance abuse problem that is dangerous to yourself and others, and can cause lasting harm or death if left untreated. It is important to note that when the problem you face involves physically harming yourself or abusing substances, you should seek the help of a licensed physician, as this book will not provide the individualized medical care you will need for these situations. Almost any event, situation, or behavior that repeatedly impacts your life negatively can be the problem you desire to fix with this method, so long as you believe it is a problem and it is causing you distressing symptoms or pain, regardless of how true or false the belief is. Once you identify the root problem, you can begin identifying why it is a problem and, eventually, how to fix it as well.

Overall, remember that the problems you face are legitimate, regardless of what anyone around you may say. Remember that you must recognize when a stressor becomes a problem by evaluating how it affects your quality of life and ability to function. By identifying what troubling conditions are hindering your life or causing symptoms of your anxiety, depression, or other negative states of mind, you put yourself one step closer to fixing the problem and healing your mental wounds. You are choosing to heal yourself and better your life, which is no small feat. Remind yourself that, however hard this process is, you will reach the light at the end of the tunnel if you keep moving forward. Your progress will soon become noticeable, a little bit at first, and soon it will be noticeable to those around you as well as you develop healthy ways of thinking. All of the pain you may uncover as you begin analyzing all of your thoughts and behaviors will be worth it.

STEP 2:

~

Identify Your Emotions, Thoughts, & Core Beliefs

Congratulations! You have discovered a list of problems that are affecting your life that you wish to change. That was a monumental step in the process. Now that you have identified the problem or problems you face, you are ready to begin parsing down how you generally feel about each situation. This is typically one of the more painful parts of the processes of cognitive behavioral therapy, as this is when you delve into how you feel about the scenario and why it hurts you or causes you discomfort. The purpose of this section is to allow you to locate the core belief that is causing disordered thinking. This is often a part of the process where many people find themselves stuck, but it is one of the most crucial as well. If you cannot identify how you feel or why you feel that way because the pain prevents you from thinking about it, or you make it a point to avoid the thoughts altogether, you will have a difficult time moving past the hurt and beginning to heal by changing how you think. Despite the pain you will feel, do not be discouraged or decide the process is not working; persevering through this challenging process will pave the way to mental wellness, and so long as you remain diligent and follow the steps provided, you will begin to see results.

In order to know how you genuinely feel and track these feelings, you may find keeping a journal, either written or verbal, useful. Free-writing may make it easier for you to track your stream of consciousness, which will allow you to easily find any patterns that may arise in that process at a glance while other people may have an easier time talking to yourself with a device or program that will record speech and convert it to text for future viewing. In the beginning, make it a point to set aside a time every day where you write or record yourself for at least a few minutes. Be sure to include any negative feelings you have felt throughout the day, as well as what you believe the trigger for those feelings may have been, regardless of how silly you may think it sounds. The goal of this activity is to identify any beliefs you hold about the specific situation that is causing your stress, as well as how you feel about it so you can discover how you think of and see yourself and your worth.

Begin by considering the problem you are facing that is negatively affecting your life. For Jane, this would look like, "My fiancé doesn't want to have children with me." Write down your problem in as simple terms as possible. It could be like Jane's, or it could be something along the lines of "My mother died," "My husband is leaving me," or "I am afraid of birds." Contemplate as deeply as possible in this stage and write down everything you can think of contributing to your recent mental distress that has been causing issues in your life. Even if you are not sure something is relevant, write it down anyway. It can't hurt to include it for analysis, but missing a key issue or pattern will hinder your healing process. It is essential to be as thorough as possible, even if you feel uncomfortable in the process.

When you have your list of problems written down, it is time to consider them individually and think about how you feel about each one. You might notice that you have a wide range of feelings about each of these problems, as the most painful tend to have layers of different emotions all mixed together. For Jane, she might decide that she feels embarrassment, anger, fear, and resentment at the situation. The man whose mother passed away may feel heartbroken, grief, anger, fear, and loneliness. The woman going through a divorce might write down that she feels scared, heartbroken, and livid, depending on the circumstances surrounding her divorce. The person with a debilitating fear of birds may write that they are ashamed, afraid, and frustrated at the aftermath caused by the thoughts surrounding birds. Include as many feelings as you have toward the problem, no matter how much you feel the emotions may contradict one another, or if you feel they are unjustified or illogical so that you can begin to parse them apart and unpack all the hurt you've been bottling up so it can start to heal. The more you have in front of you, the more material you can sift through to locate the key events and feelings, which means the better your chances at finding the root feelings and fixing them.

By identifying your feelings, you can begin to dissect the reasons you feel the way you do and search for patterns that are relevant to how you respond to stressors. By viewing patterns, you may be able to start identifying what triggers your negative response, why you respond that way, and how to correct it. Jane may look at her list of feelings and problems and notice a pattern such as she always feels distracted at work after a disagreement with her fiancé or other loved ones, no matter how insignificant the disagreement might be. The person afraid of birds may realize that they react fearfully toward any small animals that move erratically, not just birds, although birds are the most noticeable for her. Spend some time every day journaling about these stressors you are trying to correct, especially as they happen during your day-to-day life; include what happened, how you felt during and after the stressor happened, what you thought about the situation, and how you responded to it for future reference.

With your list of emotions written, it is time to identify your thoughts and beliefs about the situation. Think about when an adult confronts a dismissive teenager in an attempt to correct something. The teen might respond with a scowl, dismissively asking, "And?" over and over while the adult repeatedly tries to justify why it is important to change their behavior. Eventually, the adult gets to a point where he or she cannot continue to answer why it matters. You want to mimic this, except instead of dismissing the thoughts and feelings you come up with as irrelevant or worthless to you, you should approach each "And?" with sincerity, wanting to know the answer to your own question. You should focus on each one, noting them in your journal or whatever method you use for documentation, and continuing to parse them down until you reach an answer that tells you something about yourself. As you do these steps, make sure you write down the answer to every question you ask yourself, so when you are finished with the exercise, you can track your thoughts linearly to see how you got to the final result.

Jane writes down that her fiancé doesn't want to have children with her yet. She should then ask herself why that matters to her. "Because he doesn't want to have children with ME," she says this with emphasis on herself. And why does that matter? "Because if he doesn't want to have children with me, he might decide to have children with someone else instead." Why does that matter to you? "Because then he won't be committed to me anymore." Why does that matter? "Because I am afraid I am not good enough for him so he will go elsewhere." Note how Jane's train of thought went from how she perceives her fiancé to how she perceives herself. She has identified a core belief at the root of her problem. As you do these steps, you will watch your train of thought shift similar to Jane's, and eventually, you will reach a core belief about yourself.

A core belief is the way you feel about yourself. It defines who you are and affects everything you do in life. It affects how you perceive your surroundings and the situations in which you may find yourself involved. These beliefs largely remain entirely unconscious, but their effects permeate into every part of your life. For Jane, this belief was discovered to be the belief that she is not good enough. These may also manifest as thoughts, such as, "I am unlovable," "I am unworthy of happiness," "I am incapable of doing well," "I am a failure," "I always hurt those I love," or any other deep conviction you may hold about yourself. The previous examples are all negative core beliefs. These are all beliefs about a person and his or her worth that will cause them to act in a certain way. Someone with a core belief that always hurt people might find themselves intentionally pushing away everyone they love in an attempt to keep them from getting hurt, even though the act of pushing others away hurts them. Someone who feels they are unworthy of happiness may always put themselves last, to the detriment of their own wellbeing to the point they literally make themselves sick or deprive themselves of the necessities to make sure others are taken care of. They might sacrifice everything they want and need to make sure those around them are okay, even if that means they themselves will not be. For Jane, not being good enough means she constantly fears abandonment because she fears that someone who is good enough will come along and her fiancé or other loved ones will choose the other person over herself. This thought causes her to overanalyze any time she has a negative interaction with her loved ones. These beliefs and insecurities cause the people holding them to act in ways detrimental to their happiness, becoming a self-fulfilling prophecy and ultimately legitimizing the belief. The person believing he is unworthy of happiness sacrifices his happiness, confirming that he does not deserve it because he is not happy. Jane allows herself to get so worked up that she becomes a financial burden to her fiancé, solidifying in her mind that she is not good enough.

With that last answer Jane formed, she got to the core belief at the root of her problem: The reason she is so insecure about having children and hearing her fiancé hesitate to answer at that very moment is that she is afraid that she is not good enough. She fears that because she is not good enough, her fiancé will not wholly commit to her, and he is putting off children because he sees her as an option, but not the partner he will ultimately share his life with. After all, having children is one of the largest, permanent commitments adults will ever make, and she feels he is hesitating on making that leap with her because she is not good enough to be made into a permanent fixture in his life. Sure, they are engaged to be married, but marriages can be dissolved through a divorce. Jobs can change. Houses and other items can be bought and sold. They cannot erase having a child together; it is the ultimate commitment to one another, forever tying them together in a way that can never be undone. Rather than hearing that his reason to wait is simply finances, she latched onto the no and her anxious, self-conscious mind ran with it, playing on her insecurities and turning it into a devastating problem that had severe implications for Jane's life, relationship, and career.

As you delve into analyzing the stressful situations in your life, consider each problem individually, taking enough time to thoroughly analyze and investigate your feelings and beliefs. This process will take time, and you should not try to rush the analysis. Try focusing on one problem at a time, trying to reach the core belief, at your own pace. The beauty of this method is that you can work as quickly or slowly through the steps as you are comfortable with, and you can tailor the processes you use to your preferences. So long as you have a way to identify thoughts, feelings, and core thoughts, the how is not important. If you prefer speaking to a loved one, or writing down your feelings, or embedding them into poetry or music, so long as you can identify the feeling, thoughts, and core belief, you will be in a position to move forward in rewiring your thinking. As you get through more and more of your stressors and dissect them into thoughts, feelings, and beliefs, you may begin to identify that the same handful of core beliefs are causing a whole myriad of problems in your life and are at the root at most of your pain.

Discovering your core beliefs is an essential step toward mental wellness, as it enables you to truly understand why you behave the way you do at an unconscious level. Since core beliefs are unconscious, you react according to them without thinking, with little regard for whether it is a rational conclusion. By identifying why you react the way you do, you will be able to better understand how to avoid reacting negatively. The methods for doing so will be discussed in the next two chapters. While correcting these thoughts may seem daunting, bask in the success of making it through the process of identifying your core beliefs and feelings. It was no easy feat to manage, and only those truly dedicated to changing their lives will make it this far. Taking this process one small step at a time, one small victory at a time, makes the process seem less intimidating and allows for you to meet your goals sooner rather than later, giving you the positive reinforcement that you can, in fact, make it through this process and correct your disordered thoughts.

STEP 3:

~

Identify Inaccurate and Negative Thinking

At one point or another, everyone has experienced the self-doubt that entails when they realize something they have firmly believed was not valid. Whether they were lied to or came to the realization that their thoughts were wrong on their own, that doubt can be crippling, depending on the situation surrounding it. People feel vulnerable when their deepest thoughts are challenged and proven wrong, and naturally, they try to avoid this feeling of insecurity. So, many people, even after learning the truth, choose to double down and convince themselves that the inaccurate thought is true because being familiar is comfortable. Do not fall into this trap; understand that as painful as confronting your deepest beliefs can be, living with a healthy and accurate set of core beliefs will be worth the pain.

After discovering your list of core beliefs, it is time to start identifying either harmful or inaccurate thinking. By identifying when you are focusing on harmful or inaccurate thoughts, you can begin to make a conscious effort to correct the thoughts you have, therefore, also changing undesirable behaviors or feelings you have as a result of the thoughts. These false and negative thoughts exist to deceive you into acting or feeling in a way that may be adding fuel to the fire that is your problem, and once you can identify which ones are the deceivers, you can begin to correct them and move forward in your journey toward mental wellness.

When searching for inaccurate thinking, familiarity with formal logic can be particularly useful, as many of these inaccurate thoughts are logical fallacies; they are mistaken beliefs based on an unsound argument or reason. In simpler terms, a fallacious thought is one that you continue to believe even though there are plenty of ways to prove it false. By looking at thoughts and beliefs as logical statements to analyze as true or false, it may become easier to look at them in a detached fashion to make judgments with a clear mind. If you begin to approach your core beliefs in the way you might approach a math problem to evaluate whether it is true or false, you can begin to look objectively to judge them, detached from emotion. After all, two plus two is always four, regardless of whether you are happy, sad, or scared. By understanding what composes a negative thought or false core belief, judging them will soon become second nature. The goal of this section is to identify all of the fallacious thoughts hiding in your core beliefs so that the next section can teach you how to begin correcting them.

One of the most common fallacious thought processes is the false dilemma, or "all or nothing" thoughts. This is when you think that things must be one way or another with no middle ground. This is a black and white form of thinking that does not recognize the spectrum of greys that exist between two extremes that are not as simple as true or false statements. While a belief such as, "My favorite color is blue" is a true or false statement without a middle ground for how true or false it is, many other beliefs are not as simple. Those with these core beliefs may think that anything that is not perfection is a failure, or that not agreeing with a loved one on every single thing every single time means you do not agree on anything at all and are incompatible. If you have thoughts that present as all or nothing thoughts, they likely involve absolutes such as always or never. "I always hurt those I love," or "I will never be good enough," are two examples of this kind of thinking.

All or nothing thinking is dangerous, as you reinforce it every time it comes true. For the person who hurts those he loves, every time he hurts someone, he reinforces it. When he isn't hurting anyone, he thinks he still is due to his core belief. He then inevitably does hurt them again, whether in a petty argument or accidentally, and reaffirms that he always hurts people. He will not see the times he and his loved one had a fantastic time together or how his loved one insists that he is not the source of their pain. Any time his loved one is hurting, he automatically assumes that it must be his fault because he hurts his loved ones, regardless of whether he was the source of pain at all. For Jane, who is never good enough, she may get so caught up in every little failure that she believes that no amount of her being good enough in the eyes of others is good enough. She sees her fiancé's decision to wait on children as him indirectly saying she is not good enough to have children with, causing the situation to spiral, and reaffirming her false belief that she is not good enough, when she is, in fact, more than enough in his eyes.

Another typical distorted thought process is an overgeneralization, which goes hand-in-hand with the all-or-nothing thoughts. In this form of thinking, you latch onto one instance in which something terrible happened and then project that it will continue to happen over and over. For Jane, she may have had a defining moment as a child that caused her to feel like she is never good enough. Maybe she failed a test, or someone close to her told her that what she was doing was not good enough, and she internalized it. Even though her grades were always good and her friends always thought she was great, that one instance colored the rest of her life. For the man who hurts his loved ones, he may have done something to hurt someone once, and he locked onto that instance, ignoring all the times he helped his loved ones and made them feel wanted and loved.

The problem with this behavior is that using a small range of experiences allows for your thoughts to become quite skewed in ways they would not be if you were to look at the whole picture. It becomes all too easy to latch onto the negative, as these typically are more memorable. Our minds are hardwired to remember negative experiences and thoughts as a survival mechanism; your brain is triggered to remember the exact details that are causing your emotion. The brain does this because by focusing on the details, you will have an increased chance of survival. When you are being chased by a tiger trying to eat you, adrenaline will change how you look at the situation. You hyper-focus on the tiger, the exact details of its fangs and claws searing into your memory in hopes that the extra focus will help you somehow find a way to survive. Because of the charged negative emotions and adrenaline, your mind burns this into its memory. It sees this life-or-death situation as something worth remembering to better your chance of survival, whereas mundane day-to-day tasks or even joyful events are not necessary to remember to survive. You are more inclined to gloss over the memories that make up the vast majority of your experiences when you are met with a single negative event that contradicts the others. Jane may have been told repeatedly by her fiancé that she's fantastic, he loves her, and she is exactly perfect for him, but she ignores this reassurance in favor of her false belief that he does not want to have children with her because she is not good enough. The one time she felt inadequate for him is the time she will remember, reinforcing her negative core belief.

Many people also commonly rely on this negative emotion to pass judgment on the situation. They assume that if they have this strong negative feeling toward it, it must genuinely be a negative event, even if it could be construed as beneficial or positive. Take Jane, for example. Throughout the last few chapters, we have followed her from her argument with her fiancé over children down to identifying her core belief that she is not good enough. She would likely latch onto that one argument they had, combining it with her all-or-nothing and generalizing thinking. The negative emotion Jane feels says that she is not good enough, which compounds with the thought that she is always good enough, or never good enough, and coming to the generalization that she is never good enough from the few times she felt inadequate. Her negative feelings justify this as true in her mind.

Along these same lines, someone may magnify their negative thought or behavior, much like the saying "make mountains out of molehills." Let's say Bill drops his favorite coffee mug, shattering it and causing a big mess of coffee and glass shards. He now needs to change his clothes because he is covered in coffee, clean the dirty floor, and make a new cup for himself. While this may seem like an annoyance, for Bill, he is devastated. Bill feels like his whole day is ruined because he just added ten minutes to his morning routine, so he'll hit morning traffic on his way to work, and he'll be late. Because he is late, he will feel like anything else that happens at work happened because he was late, and suddenly, that one small event in the morning feels like this huge problem instead of a small inconvenience. Instead of seeing the mug breaking as minor, he sees it as being a defining part of his day and finds himself trapped in a negative mood for the rest of the day, and repeating the cycle every time some minor inconvenience happens, and ruining his sense of self-worth and happiness.

Along with these disordered thought patterns, there also may be some core beliefs that are simply not constructive or conducive to the situation and will not benefit you in any way if you hold onto them. While they might not fall into the previously mentioned fallacious beliefs, you may find them coloring how you feel about things unrelated to the negative thought. By repeatedly seeing the worst in every situation, you keep yourself in a negative mood, which leaves you more susceptible to fallacious thoughts such as over-generalizing that a particular weather pattern always brings certain events, or that when you hit three red lights in a row on your commute, the day will be full of challenges. Instead of seeing these as random occurrences, you pass judgment on the situation, and your negative thoughts set the stage for a negative day.

Take Jane, for example. Perhaps on the day she and her fiancé argued for the first time, it was stormy. Jane woke up that morning, looked outside, and decided it was a terrible day just because it was raining. Rain blocks the sunshine, which makes driving harder and gets her hair and clothes all wet as she walks into her office from her car. She immediately felt annoyed upon waking up and seeing the rainy weather, coloring her perception of the rest of the day when she had nothing to base that conclusion beyond an opinion. When she had her conversation with her fiancé before work, her mood was already negative, and she had already determined that day would be a bad one, making it that much easier for the day to become worse. Since it was within her expectations, she may not have taken the moment to realize that such behavior would do nothing but further ruin the day. As the day got progressively worse, she inadvertently confirmed to herself that rainy days are always bad days, but in truth, her negative thinking is what made the day bad, not the weather patterns.

By trapping yourself in a negative mood simply by letting the minor things bother you far more than they should, you do yourself a huge disservice, leaving your mental state vulnerable to negative false core beliefs that can begin to permeate into every part of your life. Remember that negativity only attracts more negativity. If you feel trapped within the cycle of negativity, you will need to learn how to begin rewiring your brain to reshape your thinking.

STEP 4:

~

Reshape Your Negative Thinking

Now that you understand how to identify when negative thinking starts to creep into your life, you can begin working to reshape your thinking altogether. The critical takeaway from this step is how to reshape your thoughts that are not conducive to mental wellness. These can be your inaccurate thoughts, fallacious thoughts, or negative thoughts, or a combination of the three. In this chapter, you will begin to understand how to adjust your mindset, and you will begin to see how drastically you can change your perspective simply by correcting harmful and inaccurate thoughts.

Just as negative thinking can color your behavior and feelings, positive thinking can do the same. Instead of looking at the downside of the situation, try to focus on the bright side, or in the case of inaccurate, fallacious thoughts, focus on the corrected thought instead. This does not mean you should try to bottle up your negative emotions and pretend they do not exist, however. While many people may think that ignoring the thinking will make it go away, this often makes the problems and intrusive thoughts worse as time goes by. There is no quick fix to negative thinking, and ignoring or drowning out the thoughts with unhealthy coping methods will not help you.

By being able to identify your negative thoughts, you will be able to identify them as they appear in real time, and you will be able to reprogram your brain to respond to the negative stimuli differently, though the process will take time and effort. By being cognizant of your thought process, you can ask yourself how to better handle the situation in the future. Jane should reflect on her situation and ask herself how she could have handled her response to her fiancé's disagreement differently. Her answer might look something like, "Instead of getting caught up in the negatives and assuming it was because I was not good enough, I could have accepted my fiancé's answer at face value and agree to revisit the conversation at a later point in time. My fiancé often tells me how perfect I am for him, so I should believe him. He has no reason to lie to me about something like this, or about his reason for not being ready to have children yet, so I should believe him." By following the steps within this book, Jane begins to recognize that the flaw in her original line of thinking is her own insecurity, and she acknowledges that she could have done things differently. By acknowledging that the negative core belief is there, but is wrong, she is not ignoring the thought or trying to bury it; instead, she is correcting it by actively reminding herself that it is wrong. Over time, with plenty of correction, Jane will eventually be able to disregard the belief that she is not good enough for her loved ones without having to consciously make an effort to see how it is an inaccurate thought. She will eventually come to accept the truth: that she is good enough the way she is.

After correcting how you could have behaved, you can begin trying to form a belief system or affirmation that you can repeat to yourself in times of weakness when you feel yourself slipping back into negative thoughts and feelings. Jane may tell herself, "I am good enough for my fiancé, and I trust him completely," when she starts feeling insecure about his behaviors and intentions, such as during a disagreement, or when she feels like she has failed him somehow. The man afraid of hurting everyone he loves may say, "Everybody makes mistakes. My presence is a genuine pleasure for many people I love." He reminds himself that he does not always hurt people, even if he accidentally does sometimes. And when he does accidentally hurt someone, he begins to recognize that humans make mistakes sometimes, and he is only human. He can begin to forgive himself for hurting his loved ones by acknowledging the mistake was nothing more than a simple mistake with an unfortunate result, and his loved ones will not shun him for an accident. You must learn to form these gentle affirmations to remind yourself that you are worthy of happiness and wellness and that your negative core beliefs do not have to permanently define who you are or how you behave.

When forming an affirmation for yourself, you must follow a set of three rules in order for it to be truly effective in correcting your beliefs. Your affirmation must be a present tense sentence. This reminds yourself that this is true at that moment, as opposed to something that was true or will be true, but might be able to be denied at the moment. By keeping it present tense, it has to be truly present tense, as you are repeating it to yourself. You can use this to ground your thinking in something positive to ward off the negative feelings that may be creeping up, or when you feel a moment of weakness or that your behavior is beginning to slip back into old habits. Your affirmation must be something to do with yourself, as you only have total control over yourself. You control how you feel or act, so you can use this to convince yourself the affirmation is valid at that moment. If your affirmation is about someone else, you cannot control it, so it becomes ineffective, or your anxious mind could plausibly deny it. Lastly, your affirmation must be constructed entirely from positive words. Leave out negative words such as not or negative forms of adjectives, such as unworthy or unhappy. The purpose of these affirmations is to solidify yourself in a positive way of thinking, which requires positive words. Just as seeing a rainy day as terrible can set you up for a day full of negativity, affirmations in negative terms keep your brain rooted in negatives as opposed to shifting to positives.

These affirmations can be tailored to virtually any situation or feeling, and you can develop them to help you make it through periods of negativity, regardless of what that negative thought is. Someone sensitive about their looks can tell themselves, "I appreciate how I look and that my body is healthy," to remind themselves to look at the positive rather than fixating on any parts of their body they dislike. Someone with anxiety could tell themselves, "I am calm and in control of my body," to remind themselves that everything is okay. You should form your affirmations to counteract whatever negative thoughts or beliefs are holding you back.

When using these affirmations, repetition is the most important factor. Take a few moments every day to recite your affirmation to yourself at least ten times in a row. You could think it, write it down, type it out in an email, sing it, include it in the art for yourself, or say it while looking at yourself in a mirror. Choose whatever method has a lasting impact on you. Any time you start feeling negative thoughts or anxiety during the day, you can repeat it back to yourself to stave off the negativity. For example, Jane could begin thinking at work about her argument with her fiancé, and rather than letting herself continue to dwell on why they had a disagreement or what her fiancé's exact words really meant, she could repeat her affirmation to herself a few times to alleviate the anxiety. As soon as she feels grounded in her positive thoughts once more, she could then move on with her day. This practice would allow her to completely by-pass the downward spiral into unproductivity that previously would hurt her every time she got distracted. Feeling confident in her positive convictions, Jane moves on. Every time she starts feeling the negativity begin to crawl back, she reminds herself once again of her affirmation. Over time, the negative thoughts are forced back, and she finds herself needing the affirmations less and less.

For many people, tying a specific part of the day to reciting their affirmations helps build the habit. The more it is done during a specific activity or time, the more it becomes second nature, like picking up your wallet before you leave home or washing your hands after using the restroom. You will begin to repeat the affirmation to yourself effortlessly, and the belief will root itself into your unconscious where it will begin to im-pact your behaviors. The goal here is to teach yourself to recite the affirmation so much that it becomes an automatic thought that overrides the negative core belief you identified earlier. This affirmation will eventually take the core belief's position, reprogramming your thinking into something positive and productive that keeps you in a state of mental wellness instead of anxiety or depression. Jane might tell herself that she is enough for her fiancé every time she is getting ready for work in the morning and in the car ride home after work, as well as every time she starts to doubt the veracity of the affirmation. While it may feel unnatural or uncomfortable at first, repeating these positive thoughts will begin to seep into other parts of your life as well, reinforcing the affirmations and slowly but surely adjusting your thinking.

With your affirmations built to begin addressing the problem from the inside out, it is time to build action plans for your most triggering situations in advance, so you have an idea of how to react. Think of this as your contingency plan in case things go wrong; just like it is easier to act in an emergency when you practice how to respond, such as having plans in case of a fire or how to perform CPR, it is easier to react healthily to a situation when you plan and prepare before the situation arises again. By being prepared, you will not get as flustered in trying to react on your feet. You will feel more in control of the situation if you have a back-up plan, which allows you to have more positive thoughts and feelings. You should begin to prepare yourself for facing your triggering situation by asking yourself how you could react in the future, as well as how you could work with your strengths or positive affirmations to react healthily.

Our friend Jane might begin to think about how to respond to her situation pragmatically, telling herself that she ought to take what her fiancé tells her at face value because he would not benefit from deceiving her, and in a healthy relationship, people do not deceive or distrust one another. If she believes that her relationship is healthy, she has to accept that anything her fiancé says is said in earnest. By admitting that she should trust her fiancé, she takes one step toward solving her issue of believing she is not good enough for him. She then tells herself that if she begins to doubt her worth, she will repeat her affirmation to herself. This affirmation will remind her that she trusts her fiancé, hopefully kicking her out of the cycle of doubting what he has to say or assigning false motives to his actions. By making a conscious effort to change her thinking, she will be able to change her behaviors. Reminding herself that she trusts her fiancé allows her to respond rationally to the situation. The next time they have a simple disagreement, Jane will be able to feel more in control of her emotions, and she will be able to accept the disagreement without it sending her into a spiral of depression.

Like Jane, you must go through the steps of writing your own action plan. Ask yourself what you can do differently the next time you feel your negative core belief rearing its ugly head. Remind yourself of things you do well that could help you the next time you face this belief head-on. Are you an avid gardener? Maybe you channel your frustration at feeling worthless toward caring for your plants, reminding yourself that you are not worthless to them and that your garden would die without you there to care for it. Do you feel like you are incapable of the most basic of tasks? Get dressed and do the dishes, then point out that you did. Instead of wallowing in the negative, redirect your feelings into something constructive that contradicts your negative belief. Write an affirmation for yourself to correct any negative habits if you notice yourself slipping into your usual behaviors. Remind yourself of your worthiness and do not short-change yourself. Take a deep breath and use these affirmations if you feel like your plan is failing, and remind yourself that this is a process that will take time. It is okay to have a slip up every now and then, and just because you slipped up does not mean you are a failure or that you should give up the process altogether.

The more you put your action plan to use, the more you should begin seeing results. As you start to feel better in certain situations and discover that these methods are working, you may find yourself more motivated than ever to continue the process and unearth more negative core beliefs that could be corrected to further better your life. The more you practice this process, the easier it gets for you to notice when your mind is going to a negative place, and the easier it gets for you to correct it with healthy thoughts and behaviors.

Reshaping your negative and inaccurate thoughts and feelings will take time, effort, and diligence, which can be discouraging for some. While you will begin to see small results relatively quickly, remember that this process is rewiring how your brain works. It is not as simple as replacing thought with another; you are literally forming new physical pathways within your brain. Every time you consciously decide to correct your negative thoughts, you strengthen these new pathways. With more and more practice, these healthy coping pathways grow stronger, which is why results take time. Just as you cannot work out once and gain six-pack abs or drop fifty pounds overnight, it takes time for your brain to form these pathways that allow for healthy thinking.

Try to think of your positive thinking as a muscle. It will start out weak, and even doing the smallest mental exercises will leave you exhausted. But with plenty of exercise and nurturing, it will grow into something stronger over time. Think of the skills provided in this book as a mental exercise. Remember that you should identify your problem, then identify your thoughts and feelings about the problem. From there, you should ask yourself why these thoughts and feelings matter to you until you discover your core beliefs. You should analyze your core beliefs, identifying which ones are negative or false, so you can identify where your mind needs work. When you have located your negative core beliefs, you should begin correcting them by planning how you could re-act better when that core belief leads to your unwanted behavior or feelings. Affirm a positive belief that replaces the negative and spending plenty of time putting these affirmations to good use while your mind rewires itself to replace the negative core belief with your affirmation.

STEP 5:

~

Set Your Goals

Throughout this entire process, you have focused on how to correct negative feelings. An equally important part of the cognitive behavioral therapy process is setting realistic goals for yourself, so you can keep yourself on track and have something attainable to strive toward. While setting goals may seem like the easiest step so far, it is tricky. Setting goals that you will be able to attain without frustrating yourself through the process can be difficult, as the standard goals people may think of regarding mental health are generally poorly chosen. Before delving into how to set a good goal, you will first learn what to avoid.

A common goal many people may try to start with is "I want to feel fulfilled with my life." This goal is trying to set an emotion. However, emotions are fleeting. No one will feel fulfilled all the time, so this is a challenging goal to reach. Any time you feel unsatisfied with your life, you may fall into the habit of thinking you cannot reach your goal, so why bother? By choosing a feeling for a goal, you set yourself up for failure because your emotions are continually adapting and changing in response to the world around you. You cannot turn emotion into a permanent state, and therefore, you should avoid goals that aim to do so to avoid a constant negative feedback loop where you consistently feel like you failed every time you do not feel the way you want to. Remember that feelings come and go, but they are just that: Feelings. Just because you feel unfulfilled does not mean it is a permanent state or that you truly are leading an unfulfilled life. In order to truly appreciate the positive sides of life, we need to feel the negatives, too. Even if you succeeded and you only ever feel a positive emotion, it becomes meaningless to you over time. You cease to appreciate it because it is your baseline and you never have anything to compare it to.

Another common, but poorly formed, goal is, "I want to be who I was before xyz event occurred." The event in this situation may change from person to person, but the result will be the same for everyone. This goal seeks to return you to your past, and because of that, is not a good goal. Unless you have a time machine, returning to the past is impossible, and you will never be who you were before because who you are is heavily influenced by your experiences. Every experience helps shape you, and they will always be a part of you. This type of goal will leave you fixated on the past and whom you used to be rather than encouraging you to grow and flourish as the individual you are now. Instead of focusing on how to heal what recent events have caused you to begin researching cognitive behavioral therapy or perhaps even seeing a therapist in an office, you focus on rewinding the clock to get a second chance at life the way you had it. Most people look back at their past from time to time and wish they could go back to other, more comfortable times, but that does not help you cope with the problem you are trying to address from the beginning. Wanting to go back would simply be running away from the problem instead of fixing it. Accepting your current situation and trying to fix that will be far more successful and beneficial to your mental wellbeing.

One last example of a poorly designed goal is "I want to avoid feeling anxiety." This seems like a good goal for someone entering therapy or trying to fix their mental state since therapy is usually to help people who have anxiety or depression stop feeling those feelings so strongly, but it still is poorly formed because it is rooted in negativity. Instead of setting a positive goal such as, "I want to develop methods for coping," it is solely rooted in removing the negative feelings altogether. Wanting to stop feeling anxious in certain situations can cause aversions to those specific situations to develop; an individual may become fixated on avoiding known anxiety triggers to avoid the anxiety altogether, which may make the situation worse. By wanting to stop the anxiety, you may go out of your way to avoid any situation that could potentially cause anxiety to begin with. After all, avoiding the situation means meeting your goal, right? Wrong. You only make your anxiety worse by trying to avoid it rather than facing it head-on. You become preoccupied with avoiding your anxiety triggers simply because you are anxious about avoiding anxiety, and if you feel anxiety in response to many day-to-day tasks, this may leave you avoiding necessary actions or events, or causing you to miss out on the things you enjoy. For example, if driving brings you anxiety, and your goal is to avoid anxiety, the natural solution is to avoid driving. However, if you live in an area with very few options for public transportation, you find yourself trapped at home, which may make your anxiety worse as you miss out on things that you enjoy.

Now that you have an understanding of what a lousy goal looks like, you are ready to avoid the traps these goals set, and set goals that will actually be beneficial to your mental health and your life. Start by considering things that bring you joy or are important to you. These can be related to hobbies or your health, so long as they bring value to your life in one form or another. Your goals are there to help you better yourself, so you ought to make them something you value. By choosing goals that are important to you, you are more rewarded by achieving them, not only because you completed a goal, but also because the act of completing your goal also made you feel better. With a general idea of a goal in mind, it is time to get more specific. Many life coaches and therapists like to use the SMART method to set goals for their clients. SMART stands for Specific, Measurable, Achievable, Realistic, and Timed. If you remember to set SMART goals, you will find yourself with goals that are easier to achieve and plan, setting you up for success.

The first step in identifying your goal is to be specific. Think about what you would like to accomplish. This could be anything from getting more exercise to setting up a time for your favorite hobby, keeping a diary, or writing a book. This could also be related to your mental health, such as developing coping mechanisms for anxiety or filling out a gratitude journal to help you remember all of the things you appreciate in your life in an attempt to help with your depression. Anything that benefits you in an impactful way will work here, so long as the action is specific and you value the action. The more specific you make your goal in this section, the easier it will be to meet since you will have an idea of what your completed goal will look like. Instead of setting a goal of "I want to get healthier," you specify, "I want to lose weight and increase my stamina." This is a step in the right direction, but can be made even more specific: "I want to lose ten pounds and be able to run an eight-minute mile." The goal with the specified weight and time limit for a mile has a much clearer finish line than just losing weight or increasing stamina.

Next, you will make the goal measurable. This part is simple: If your goal is to exercise, you can say you want to work out three times a week. For writing in a journal, it could be daily. If your goal is reconnecting with your significant other through more date nights, you could set this part as monthly. It could also be writing a certain amount each day or spending an hour a day to yourself without having to care for others. So long as you specify how often or how much of something you will do the steps to work toward your goal, you will meet this requirement.

The goal should be easily achievable, with smaller sub-goals set in the beginning to help you stay on track. The more often you meet your goals, the better you will feel about yourself, and the better you feel about yourself, the more likely you are to continue pursuing the goals. For this reason, setting small milestones for yourself can keep you on track. If your goal is to write a book, which you will work on five days a week, you could set a smaller goal of writing 1,000 words a day until your book is complete. These smaller goals will make the big goal seem much less daunting. To the person saying he wants to lose ten pounds and run an eight-minute mile, he could set that he will run two miles a day during his workouts with the hopes of dropping 30 seconds from his time a week.

Your goal needs to be realistic for you. What is realistic can be one of the trickier parts to identify, as what is realistic for one person may not be realistic for another. For some, writing a book would be easy, but for others, it could be like pulling teeth. Likewise, for some people, playing a sport or exercising regularly would be simple, but others are incapable, due to injury or disability. Remember, your goal should be something that will bring you joy or will provide value to your life somehow, and while it will likely be a challenge of sorts, you should avoid setting yourself up for failure by assigning a goal that you are likely trying to avoid. If you are out of shape, you likely will not be able to run a marathon after a month, and likewise, most people are incapable of shedding a large amount of weight in a week. Setting a difficult or near-impossible goal will only hinder your progress and discourage you from continuing when you see that your progress is not where you would like it to be.

You should also set a reasonable amount of time for you to complete your goal. Again, make this a realistic time for whatever your goal is. If you want to write a book and agree to write it 1,000 words a day, it will take you a few months to finish it, and that is okay. Likewise, a goal such as learning a new art technique might be a more short-term goal. Setting a variety of short and long-term goals may help you remain motivated, as you always have something to strive for, and you are always reaching the goals you have set, encouraging you to continue trying to strive for your long-term goals.

Now that you understand the basics of what makes a goal good, you can begin applying these new skills to yourself to help your mental health. Our friend Jane may set a goal saying, "I want to be entirely comfortable with my fiancé, so he no longer triggers my anxiety." Looking at that goal, it seems rather abstract, and would need to be broken down into smaller goals, such as, "I want to have a date night every Thursday for the next two months with my fiancé, where each week, we choose an activity that requires a great deal of cooperation with one another to complete." This goal is specific: they will have regular dates. It is measurable: they do it every Thursday night for the next two months. It is achievable: it gives them a small number of times to complete the desired behavior before the goal has been satisfied. It is realistic: if Jane and her fiancé are free every Thursday, there is no reason they cannot succeed in meeting the goal. It is timed: they know they are done after a certain number of date nights that are held at specific times. With Jane's SMART goal, she can foster an even deeper relationship with her fiancé. Since their activities require plenty of cooperation such as dancing together, playing tennis, or doing a joint painting class where each of them paints half of the picture, Jane learns she has to be comfortable with him and trust him in order to meet their small goals, all while doing things she genuinely enjoys with her fiancé. As a result, she gets more comfortable with him and trusts him, while also working through the steps to rewire negative or inaccurate thoughts. Over time, as she completes her date nights and follows steps one through four in this book to consciously correct her negative thoughts, she will begin to find that she stops worrying about whether she is good enough for him.

For the best effect, create goals that go hand-in-hand with your positive affirmations. Jane's affirmation to trust her fiancé goes hand-in-hand with her goal of dates that require their cooperation and trust to accomplish. As she completes each date night, she reinforces that she can trust and rely on him without questioning motives, which reinforces her initial affirmation. When she begins to feel reluctant to trust her partner, such as during a dance class date, she can repeat her affirmation of "I trust my fiancé completely," to remind her that her fiancé will both literally and figuratively catch her as she falls. By going through with the dip and also being caught by her partner, she reinforces the truth of her affirmation and is slightly more likely to remember that she can trust him the next time she feels her insecurities getting the best of her. As her affirmations and goals work together, she continues to exercise her brain's new pathways and reinforce positive thinking. As Jane continues to use the skills she has been practicing to help her identify other flawed core beliefs, she begins to nurture a healthier mindset that brings her happiness and security.

STEP 6:

~

Identify Your Obstacles

Every process with significant results has obstacles that make it challenging to complete. Nothing in life is free. Significant results are not easy, and usually, things are hard because they have plenty of obstacles blocking the path to success. Therapeutic processes involving rewiring your thoughts are no exception, and along the road, you will likely meet many obstacles that may discourage you or make you feel like you should quit. This section will teach you which common obstacles you may face, as well as how to work around them to get the most out of your effort and begin seeing results despite the setbacks.

A common obstacle many people face is feeling shame at having issues, to begin with. These people feel ashamed of the fact that they are not coping with the way others think they should, and this hinders their healing. Instead of addressing the source of their shame, people try to bury it down deeper to avoid the humiliation of admitting they have a problem, to begin with. These people get so caught up in the fact that they know their thoughts are wrong or unhealthy that they cannot get past the shame of admitting they have a problem. Perhaps, a man grew up being told, "Boys don't cry; pull yourself up by your bootstraps and get it together," and was punished every time he showed signs of perceived weakness. He grew up learning to hide his emotions, as if they were a source of shame, instead of learning to reach out and ask for help when it is needed. The problem with this logic is that it is literally physically impossible to pull yourself up by your bootstraps. The phrase itself used to be employed sarcastically, describing something impossible to do. When the man grew up being told to pull himself up, he was being told to do something impossible, and he learned to be ashamed of the inevitable failure. He knew he was failing, and found himself embarrassed by it, and grew up to be a man afraid of seeking help or admitting he has a problem because a problem means he failed to be a man.

Instead of being told to deal with it, he would have been better served with a reminder that everyone has feelings, and everyone makes mistakes. Despite what he may have been taught to believe, no one will look at him as less of a man if he needs help learning to cope with his feelings. If anything, the fact that he was never taught as a child means that he needs the help even more. In order to get past the shame, you should start by setting small, attainable goals that break away the shame you feel bit by bit. Remind yourself that it is okay to need help, and you are not the first, nor will you be the last, to need it. Recognize that your friends and family will be just as happy to help you as you would be to help them in a time of need. And just as it is acceptable to seek help when you break a leg, it is acceptable to seek help when you feel like part of your mental health needs healing as well.

Another common obstacle is the fear of the unknown. People crave comfortable and familiar, so they will naturally gravitate what they know. Even when what they know is pain, depression, and anxiety, it is still familiar to them, and at some level, they cling to it regardless of the consequences. These people fear who they will be without their negative thoughts, especially for those who have lived with those negative thoughts and feelings their entire lives. No one wants to feel like they do not know who they are as a person, even if that means that they consequentially live unhappily.

For those with this mindset, following the steps listed in parts one through four may be helpful. When identifying that what you feel is fear, you can begin to ask yourself why you fear it. As you get through your feelings on the situation and recognize why you are afraid, you can look at the consequences of remaining in a fearful state as opposed to working past it. Sure, you do not entirely know who you will be when you let go of your negativity, but are you happy with who you are as is? It might be familiar, but is your life satisfying? If you are reading this book, the answer to this question is probably no. Despite the discomfort you feel, remember to use the steps in this book. Create a gentle affirmation for yourself, such as, "I am worthy of happiness, and I will always treat myself with love, even when it is tough." Every time you start to feel afraid of the process, whether it is because of the pain of parsing through your trauma, or because you are afraid of not knowing who you will be when you are done, remind yourself that you will treat yourself with love. You deserve the treatment that will help you become mentally healthy, and you deserve to be happy. Even if the process is tough, if the result will be shifting to a positive way of thinking, it will help bring you happiness.

People often feel overwhelmed when they start the process of therapy, and that sensation of being overwhelmed discourages them from continuing. When you do not know where to start, it is difficult to dive in and begin. Just like it can be overwhelming to try to get into a new career line because of everything it entails and not knowing where to begin looking, it can be challenging to begin unpacking your mental state, especially when you have a lifetime of disordered thinking to parse through.

This overwhelmed feeling deters many people from wanting to continue with the process, and because they never actually get started, they remain stuck in their state of negativity, feeling overwhelmed every time they try to unpack. In order to get past this overwhelming sensation, think of it as a river. You can either fight the current and try to swim upstream, or you can choose to ride the current and let it carry you forward. While it is not pleasant to get through the period of feeling overwhelmed, this feeling enables you to know that it is something that needs to be addressed, even if you need help in doing so. Embrace the current and let it carry you forward, even though it will hurt at first. Wounds hurt as they heal, and your mental wounds are no different. You can give yourself an affirmation to keep you grounded when you begin to feel overwhelmed such as, "I will persevere and work toward mental health and happiness. This feeling will pass, and the end result will be worthwhile." Every time you begin feeling like you want to quit, you can remind yourself that the pain is a temporary, but necessary part of the process. If healing your thought processes was easy, no one would be in the position of needing to read self-help books or get therapy to help them, and mental illness and disordered thinking would not exist.

The last common obstacle you may face is yourself. You, yourself, may impose limits that hold you back during the process of trying to correct your thinking. A lot of times, this is entirely unconscious, and people do not even realize they are doing it. This type of self-scan can be as innocuous as telling yourself, "I will never be able to do something like that," when they see someone expertly unicycling down the road, or watch a chef prepare a meal in front of them. While they may be correct in saying they will never be able to do that, they are still limiting themselves. By setting a limit, they may not ever try to surpass it. Likewise, people may develop habits of focusing on things they believe they can never do, and it eventually creates a very self-defeating person. By truly believing that, even with time, dedication, and hard work, you will never be able to do something, you will not see the point in at least trying, and this can have a very detrimental effect in trying to change your mindset. It is not a far reach to go from, "I will never be able to get that degree," to "I will never be happy with my life." Just like you may feel like you should not attempt the degree because it will be a waste of time and energy, you may feel like making an effort to become a more positive person will waste your time and energy as well, so there is no point in even attempting it.

In order to work past this sort of self-defeating attitude, you must again apply the methods described in parts one through four.

Remember, those negative thoughts are not beneficial to you. Self-defeating thoughts are equally as unbeneficial. Instead, you should focus on positive thoughts. Every time you find yourself thinking in absolutes, stop yourself and remind yourself that with enough effort, you might be able to succeed. Of course, you cannot succeed at literally everything you ever set out to do, but that does not mean you should avoid trying. Trying and failing is a step toward success. After all, some of the most successful, influential people in the world have failed repeatedly before becoming successful. J.K. Rowling, broke, newly divorced, and struggling to survive and care for her child, submitted the first Harry Potter book dozens of times before it was accepted and published. Through perseverance, she has become one of the most well-known authors in recent time. She probably thought that she would never get published during low points, but through trying repeatedly, she met a goal that likely felt impossible to her along the way. You, too, should remember that limiting yourself will only impose limits that were never there, to begin with. Much of our modern world was once deemed impossibility, until one day, it became possible. We used to think traveling long distances was impossible until we tamed horses and used them to help us travel quicker, and eventually made cars to travel even quicker than horses could. Never set negative limits for yourself; they will only serve to hinder you.

Now that you are aware of these obstacles, as well as how you could potentially work through them, you will be less likely to succumb to them. By knowing ahead of time what difficulties you will face, you will be better prepared. Remember that these obstacles will be painful to navigate through, but the pain is temporary. With the skills provided to you through this guide, you will be equipped to work your way through the obstacles and reach mental health.

Conclusion

Congratulations on making it to the end of this book! You have now learned the steps you will need to begin rewiring your brain to heal from depression, anxiety, phobias, or any other kinds of disordered thinking.

Regardless of your reasoning for picking up this book, the methods in this book will help you return to a healthier way of thinking. By shifting your thoughts from harmful and counterproductive to wellbeing to positive, you will begin to see improvements in your mood and life. As your brain develops new pathways for thinking, you will feel your personality grow and flourish.

Remember the steps in correcting your thoughts and behavior. You must first identify the problems you feel are affecting your life. You must identify your emotions and thoughts, continuing to delve deeper and deeper into them until you reach your core values, which are the unconscious beliefs about yourself that shape everything you do and feel. When you have identified your beliefs, you must begin to identify which thoughts and beliefs are false or harmful. These are the beliefs that will deceive you and keep you trapped in a cycle of negative thinking, and you must become aware of the traps to avoid them. With the false, negative beliefs identified, you must begin reshaping your thinking through the process of identifying alternative ways of thinking positive affirmations to solidify the alternate ways of thinking, and setting up an action plan to be able to better cope with situations in the future when you find yourself slipping into past behavior. You must set goals that will help affirm your positive ways of thinking and begin to create positive core beliefs for yourself. By following these steps, you will set yourself on the path to rewiring your brain and altering your thoughts.

Remember, like with learning any new skill or breaking any bad habit, you will have to put in plenty of effort. You will face roadblocks as you make progress. It may feel like you are not making any progress at all as you feel pain or discouragement, but do not forget that each and every step is a milestone of its own, and in moments of weakness, remind yourself that the negative feelings will pass. Look back at the progress you have made, whether it was through journaling or on your own, and see how far you have come. Even just recognizing that you have a thought system that needs correcting is a significant first step in the right direction. With effort, you will succeed, and if you feel unequipped to do so yourself, you can identify friends, family, or even a therapist in your area that will be able to help you. Mental wellness is within your reach, so long as you put in the work and seek the help you need. Remain motivated in your endeavors, and remember, you are worthy of happiness. You are worthy of living a life that brings you fulfillment. You are lovable. You are worth the effort to improve your mental wellbeing.